Brighton Trolleybuses

Andrew Henbest
Series editor Robert J Harley

MP *Middleton Press*

Cover Picture: This is a scene that thousands of visitors and residents alike will remember of Brighton's fast, silent and non-polluting trolleybuses, for they were part of the transport scene from immediately prior to the Second World War to the early 1960s. On a gloriously sunny day in the late 1950s, Corporation AEC trolleybus no. 21 is just about to depart on its circular route to the London Road shops, then climb to the residential areas beyond, terminating at Preston Drove. Corporation no. 43 of the same type will follow to St Peter's Church, then branch off to serve the relatively flat Lewes Road as far as the Barracks. This view shows the Old Steine terminus which was the hub of the system and is unusual as Corporation trolleybuses normally carried two advertisements either side of the front destination screen. Just across the road is the Aquarium, the Palace Pier and Brighton's beaches. (J.Copland / Photobus)

Published September 2005

ISBN 1 904474 34 9

© *Middleton Press, 2005*

Design Emily Pede

Published by
    Middleton Press
    Easebourne Lane
    Midhurst, West Sussex
    GU29 9AZ
Tel: 01730 813169
Fax: 01730 812601
Email: info@middletonpress.co.uk
www.middletonpress.co.uk

Printed & bound by Biddles Ltd, Kings Lynn

CONTENTS

INTRODUCTION AND ACKNOWLEDGEMENTS

I am delighted to have the opportunity to provide this pictorial history of trolleybuses in my home town of Brighton. I grew up in the Brighton suburb of Woodingdean in the 1950s and 1960s with my two younger sisters, and while not living on a trolleybus route, from time to time I travelled on both Brighton, Hove and District and Brighton Corporation trolleybuses when going about everyday activities. Brighton trolleybuses were an important part of life from my earliest years.

My sincere thanks are due to the photographers who had the foresight to travel the system and take the many excellent views seen in this book. None are my own, for I was too young to be able to take photographs, let alone afford a camera or film. Where possible, individual photographers have been acknowledged, but in some cases I do not know who took the photograph. I apologise for this omission and hope that the individuals concerned will derive the satisfaction of knowing that their work has made an invaluable contribution to this publication. I thank Ken Allbon for supplying a copy of the system map and for his fine drawings of the trolleybuses themselves. I also thank series editor Robert Harley, fellow Brighton trolleybus enthusiasts Eric Bristoll, Mervyn Stedman, Roger Ticehurst, Peter Williams and Brighton historian, Chris Horlock, all of whom allowed me access to their photograph collections. I also acknowledge the work of other students of the Brighton trolleybus system whose work I have referred to in order to write the historical information. These are David Kaye and Martin Nimmo's *The Trolleybuses of Brighton and Hove*, R.Knight's *Brighton Corporation Transport Fleet History*, John Roberts' *British Bus and Trolleybus Systems (no. 4) Brighton Hove and District* and Peter Ticehurst and Alan Piatt's *From Tramshed to Go-Ahead*. I have also referred to local newspapers including *The Sussex Daily News*, the *Evening Argus* and the *Brighton and Hove Herald* and to other sources, including John Gillham's article on Brighton Trolleybus Abandonment in *Buses illustrated* (July 1959), his fine system map and to Anthony Dale's *About Brighton*. I am also grateful to Ken Allbon, Tony Carder, Mervyn Stedman, Peter Williams and my daughter Marian for their helpful comments when proof reading the text. Finally to my wife, Linda and younger daughter, Christine for giving me encouragement and help in the writing of this book.

The timetables reproduced herein are from Brighton, Hove and District Transport's Bus Timetable and Map, Winter issue 1958-59.

Andrew P. Henbest,
Worthing. May 2005

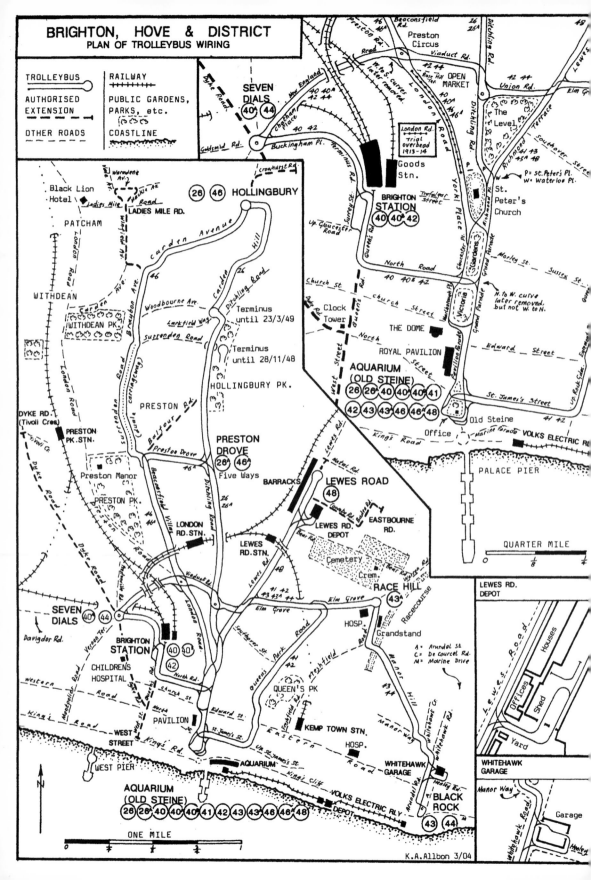

GEOGRAPHICAL SETTING

Brighton and the neighbouring town of Hove are located on the south coast of England, a little over 50 miles (80 kilometres) from London. The town, once the small fishing village of Brighthelmstone, grew into a fashionable seaside resort following the discovery that sea bathing was good for the health. Brighton prospered from the second half of the eighteenth century after Prince Regent, later to become George IV, built his holiday palace - the Royal Pavilion - there. The four and a half miles (seven kilometres) of beach is made up of pebbles from the Hove - Portslade boundary in the west, to Black Rock in the east, but at low tide a sandy strip is often uncovered. The Chalk on which Brighton is built rises steeply to the north and east - the highest point of the South Downs in the area is reached at Ditchling Beacon, which is 813 feet (248 metres)

above sea level. Two deep, dry river valleys cut through the Chalk, meander roughly north-west and north-east from the old town. Along these valleys are the main transport links to Crawley and London in the north, and Lewes, Eastbourne and Hastings in the east. The sea-front route to the bridging points of the river Adur at Shoreham-by-Sea in the west is relatively flat by comparison, leading to Worthing, Chichester and beyond. Within the town itself the dry valleys ensure that Brighton is dominated by steep hills to which the trolleybuses were ideally suited. Indeed, on gradients such as Braybon Avenue, Ditchling Road, Elm Grove and Manor Hill, the silent acceleration and speed of fully laden trolleybuses was quite breathtaking, never being surpassed by any other public transport vehicles, before or since.

HISTORICAL BACKGROUND

The story of Brighton's trolleybuses goes back to the early years of the twentieth century. At this time, the area's public transport system was run by the horse trams of Brighton and Shoreham Tramway Company Limited, the electric trams of Brighton Corporation Tramways and the horse and motor buses of Brighton, Hove and Preston United Omnibus Company Limited. (The history of the trams has already been covered in *Brighton's Tramways* first published in October 1992 as part of the Tramway Classics series.) The latter company had operated some battery-powered buses from June 1909 and although they were more costly to operate and maintain than petrol buses, their silence and comfortable running were popular features. The success of these electric buses led to the idea of using trackless trolley vehicles and on 2nd August 1911, the Company obtained an Act of Parliament to enable it to operate a number of trackless trolley vehicle routes in Brighton and Hove. A further trolleybus Bill in 1912 sought powers for other routes in Brighton, but Brighton Corporation and Hove Corporation persuaded the Company to withdraw the Bill. Both municipalities however obtained Acts of Parliament on 7th August 1912 to operate trolleybuses on routes within their boundaries

and on joint routes linking both boroughs.

When there were proposals to co-ordinate the various transport undertakings in the Brighton and Hove area in the 1930s, trolleybuses were again mentioned and Brighton Corporation decided to seek powers to operate them. The Brighton Corporation Transport Act (1938) became operative from 1st April 1939 and was effective for 21 years. It allowed the Corporation tramways to be replaced by buses or trolleybuses. Traffic revenues were to be shared and miles were to be operated in the proportions of 72.5% to the Brighton, Hove and District Omnibus Company, and 27.5% to the Corporation, each paying its own running costs. Both were required to provide sufficient buses and trolleybuses to operate their share of the services. The Corporation was to own all the fixed trolleybus equipment and receive payment from the Company for its use. However, the operation of trolleybuses was restricted to the Borough of Brighton. All the vehicles used were as far as practicable to be of the same standard, carrying capacity and colour and bearing the words Brighton, Hove and District Transport.

The Corporation appointed a new General Manager and Engineer, Winston Robinson, AMIAE, AMInstT, to supervise the changeover from trams to buses. The modification of the tramway's electrical supply and the erection of the trolleybus overhead wiring for the 550V system was awarded to Clough, Smith and Co Ltd, London. The firm began to convert the tramway overhead equipment for trolleybus operation starting on 1st February 1939. The Company took up its option to provide one fifth of the trolleybus fleet and ordered eight almost identical vehicles in 1939.

The first of the trolleybuses arrived in Brighton on 30th March 1939. Number 1 (FUF 1) made a trial run in the early hours of Friday morning, 31st March 1939 when the streets were deserted and the trams had gone back to the depot. The trolleybus made its first public appearance in daylight on Monday, 3rd April 1939 – a photograph appeared in the local newspaper, the Evening Argus on Maundy Thursday, 6th April. By this time the conversion programme had begun and the first tram route withdrawal (route M – Lewes Road and Seven Dials) had taken place. The trolleybuses were put into immediate use for driver training purposes and it was hoped that there would be enough vehicles available to operate completely the Lewes Road, Ditchling Road and Beaconsfield Road tram routes after an inaugural ceremony booked for Whit Monday, 1st May 1939.

As it turned out, the inaugural ceremony was postponed by a month, but as from Monday, 1st May 1939 the third part of the reorganisation scheme took place, this time involving the trolleybuses. The existing Lewes Road tram service, L, between Old Steine and the Barracks was withdrawn and replaced by new route 48 trolleybuses running from Aquarium, Old Steine to the Barracks (Lewes Road) via Victoria Gardens, St Peter's Church and Lewes Road every 4-5 minutes. The first trolleybus to run in. The editor was most complimentary towards the trolleybuses. The difference for the general public must have been quite amazing for, compared with the trams and many buses of the day, the trolleybuses were state-of-the-art vehicles built to a high standard including decorative Alhambrinal ceiling panels and features such as enclosed staircases and roofs! The bodywork was particularly handsome and was enhanced by the striking red and cream livery adopted for the new joint fleet.

The final part of the conversion programme took place on 31st August 1939 when trams ran on routes E (to Elm Grove) and Q (to Queen's Park Road) for the last time. With the streets deserted the last of Brighton's trams (car 41) ran into the depot carrying civic dignitaries at around 1am the following morning. Starting on Friday, 1st September there were four new trolleybus services, each running every ten minutes. Brighton's trams to trolleybuses conversion made history in that it had been completed in just four months.

During August and September, Brighton, Hove and District's eight trolleybuses 6340-7 (BPN 340-7) were delivered to the Company's Conway Street Garage in Hove. However, before they could be placed in service or any further expansion of the trolleybus system could take place, war was declared on 3rd September 1939. The Company trolleybuses were put into store at Whitehawk Garage, their registrations were surrendered and the Whitehawk extension was postponed.

The enforcement of night-time 'blackout' conditions caused a number of accidents as all vehicles were fitted with masks over their headlamps. Interior lighting was also reduced which made life extremely difficult for conductors. Eight of the trolleybuses (nos. 1-8) received an all-over khaki livery and were parked each night outside at The Level while other vehicles were parked outside the garage in Lewes Road itself. Roofs were painted grey as a form of camouflage against air attack. As young men joined the armed forces, staffing became difficult and so the Corporation employed female trolleybus conductors and drivers. Mrs Nora Miller was the first woman to drive trolleybuses in Brighton. To assist passengers in the blackout, no. 16 was fitted with a light on the rear platform that illuminated as it stopped. 'Vehicle in motion' signs lit up as it started moving again.

Many children were evacuated from the Brighton and Hove area during the war and in May 1942 the Corporation sent five or six trolleybuses (nos. 11-15 and possibly no. 10 as well) to Newcastle-upon-Tyne where there was a greater demand for them. After a brief period of operation, they returned to Brighton during September and October. Considerable damage to property was caused by an air raid on 25th May 1943. The doors and windows of Whitehawk Garage were damaged in a series of blasts, but fortunately the eight stored trolleybuses escaped any damage. The future of these trolleybuses was discussed during 1944. It was decided that the Company should negotiate with the Corporation to take up its option of operating them rather than let its powers lapse. Agreement was reached in July 1944 to introduce the trolleybuses gradually to the system. The Corporation accordingly trained a number of Company bus drivers and an electrician (at the Company's expense) in order for this to happen. Initially three vehicles were moved from Whitehawk to Lewes Road Garage for electrical testing by the manufacturers. 6342 was registered CPM 53 and licensed for driver training purposes on 17th October 1944, while 6340 and 6341 were registered CPM 61-2 respectively and licensed from 1st November 1944. These were almost certainly the first trolleybuses to reappear with cream roofs.

With a return to peacetime conditions, work began on the extension of trolleybus wiring from the Race Hill to Black Rock. Work had progressed well enough to enable Company trolleybuses to be based at their Whitehawk Garage from 17th February 1946. Trolleybus route 44 was extended to Black Rock from Sunday, 3rd March 1946, the day that the Company completely took over the operation of this route. The Corporation jointly worked route 43A, which was extended beyond the Race Hill on summer weekends as route 43. All other routes were worked by the Corporation, with the exception of one duty on routes 41 / 42 from June to December 1946. The last of the stored Company trolleybuses, 6347 was registered CPM 997 and entered service from 1st May 1946.

On 6th October 1947, it was agreed to extend the trolleybus system into the developing Hollingbury estate and both overhead and vehicles were ordered – eight by the Corporation and three by the Company. The three Company vehicles arrived as 6391-3 (DNJ 992-4) in March 1948 and were put to work on route 44. Six Corporation vehicles 45-50 (HUF 45-50) arrived in March – April 1948 with two chassis put into store

On 28th November 1948, routes 26 and 46 were extended up Ditchling Road onto the edge of the Hollingbury estate to a turning circle at Larkfield Way. These routes were again extended into the estate on 23rd March 1949 via Carden Hill to a turning circle at Carden Avenue but the Summer Sunday extension of route 43A to Black Rock as route 43 finished in 1950. The final extension took effect on 12th August 1951 when route 46 was diverted from Beaconsfield Villas and ran to Hollingbury via Surrenden Road, Braybon Avenue and Carden Avenue. This brought the route mileage to a maximum of 14.54 miles (23.4 km).

Following successful trials during 1951, both the Company and Corporation changed from using a 'Bell Punch' non-geographical pre-printed ticket system to using 'Ultimate' machines with rolls of pre-printed coloured tickets.

The stored pair of trolleybuses entered service as 51-2 (LCD 51-2) on 25th March 1953, bringing the joint fleet to a maximum of 63 - the Corporation owning 52 and the company just 11.

By 1954, a Transport sub-committee had been set up to report on the working of the joint agreement. The Special Transport Committee recommended that the Corporation should seek permission to run three new services to the developing Woodingdean estate to the east of the town. The cost of extending the trolleybus network to Woodingdean was estimated at £40,000; failure to do so would mean losing revenue on existing services 41, 42, 43A and 44 to these new routes. The Committee asked the Corporation whether the trolleybuses would be retained or replaced with motorbuses. On Thursday, 27th September 1956 Brighton Council voted unanimously to replace trolleybuses gradually with motorbuses. The Special Transport Committee began work on revising the 1938 agreement while the Advisory Committee made plans for the abandonment of the trolleybus system. It was decided that the trolleybuses would be replaced in two stages and in due course twenty Leyland motorbuses were ordered by the Corporation.

Stage One of the trolleybus replacement programme took place on Tuesday, 24th March 1959. This was the last day that trolleybuses worked on routes 41, 42, 43A, 44 and 48. No. 342 (CPM 53) was the last Company trolleybus in service - it worked the 11.24 pm service from Aquarium, Old Steine to Whitehawk Garage with ten passengers on board.

The final day of trolleybus operation was fixed for Friday, 30th June 1961. This was a hot, sunny day and 14 of the 23 trolleybuses available were in operation – AECs 1, 4, 6, 17, 20, 23, 27, 33, 34, 35, 36, 38, 43 and 44. The last trolleybus in service was no. 36 driven by Wally Levitt with Fred Bracey conducting. The trolleybuses had carried some 465 million passengers during their 22-year reign and had collected £4 million in revenue.

CHRONOLOGY OF
TROLLEYBUS ROUTES

1st May 1939   Brighton's first trolleybus route opened
    48 Aquarium, Old Steine – Barracks (Lewes Road)

1st June 1939   Official inauguration of the trolleybus system
    New trolleybus routes
    26 Aquarium, Old Steine – Ditchling Road (Surrenden Road) via Open Market
    46 Aquarium, Old Steine – Ditchling Road (Surrenden Road) via Beaconsfield Villas
    26A Aquarium, Old Steine – Preston Drove via Open Market
    46A Aquarium, Old Steine – Preston Drove via Beaconsfield Villas

22nd June 1939   New trolleybus route
    40A Aquarium, Old Steine – Seven Dials via London Road

17th July 1939   New trolleybus routes
    40 Aquarium, Old Steine – Aquarium, Old Steine via London Road, Seven Dials
    and Brighton Station
    40B Aquarium, Old Steine - Brighton Station (occasional peak Summer journeys)

1st September 1939
    40A Service withdrawn being effectively replaced by 42
    New trolleybus routes -
    41 Aquarium, Old Steine – Aquarium, Old Steine via Richmond Terrace, Elm
    Grove, Queen's Park Road and St James's Street
    42 Brighton Station – Brighton Station via Seven Dials, Open Market,
    Elm Grove, Queen's Park Road, St James's Street and Old Steine
    43A Aquarium, Old Steine – Race Hill via Richmond Terrace and Elm Grove
    44 Seven Dials – Race Hill via Open Market and Elm Grove

8th September 1939
    42 Clockwise route diverted to operate via Aquarium, Old Steine terminus

18th September 1939
    Wartime cut - 40 Service withdrawn

3rd March 1946   44 Service extended to Black Rock via Manor Hill
    43A Summer extension to Black Rock via Manor Hill as route 43

28th November 1948
    26 and 46 Both services extended to Larkfield Way

23rd March 1949 26 and 46 Both services extended to Hollingbury (Carden Avenue) via Carden Hill

Summer 1950   43 Service not worked regularly after this time, but the number 43 was used for
    last journeys to Whitehawk Garage

12th August 1951 46 Service diverted at Beaconsfield Villas to operate to Hollingbury (Carden
    Avenue) via Surrenden Road, Braybon Avenue and Carden Avenue

Summer 1955   40B Route number not used after this time

24th March 1959 Last day of Brighton, Hove and District trolleybuses
    41, 42, 43A, 44 and 48 Services replaced and / or revised to operate with
    motorbuses
    The number 48 was used for last journeys to Lewes Road Garage
    (Final use of number 43)

30th June 1961   Last day of Brighton Corporation trolleybuses
    26, 26A, 46 and 46A Services replaced and / or revised to operate with
    motorbuses
    (Final use of number 48)

EARLY EXPERIMENTS WITH TROLLEYBUSES

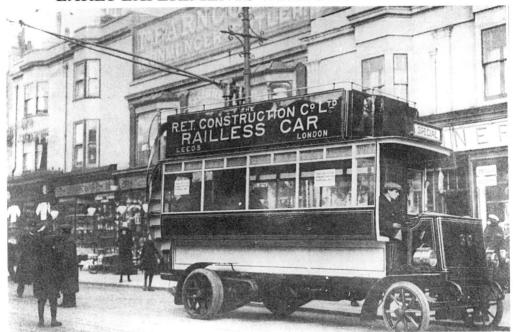

1. This RET Construction Co Ltd Railless Car was the first trolleybus to operate in Brighton between December 1913 and January 1914. It was demonstrated to Brighton and Hove Councils on a number of occasions using 690 yards of wiring that had been erected in London Road, shown here between Rose Hill Terrace and Trafalgar Street. (East Pennine Transport Group – R.Marshall coll.)

2. Although this book is about Brighton's trolleybuses, Hove Corporation's experimental trackless trolley vehicle cannot be ignored. It has attracted quite a crowd, mainly of cyclists and is seen in Goldstone Villas undergoing trials in September 1914. Power was brought from the Cedes-Stoll overhead system to the vehicle, by means of a flexible cable attached to a four-wheeled over-running trolley. Although Acts of Parliament were obtained to run trolleybuses in both Brighton and Hove and the tests were a total success, none of the proposals was realised and this vehicle was destined to be the only trolleybus to operate in Hove. (Pamlin Prints)

TROLLEYBUSES ON TRIAL

3. When there were proposals to co-ordinate the various transport undertakings in the Brighton and Hove area, a demonstration trolleybus route was erected at The Level. Portsmouth's new trolleybus no. 20 (RV 6378) was hired for a week and made its first trip on 12th December 1935. It is seen here among the crowds that had gathered to witness the event.
(Brighton Herald Ltd)

4. London Transport's centre entrance trolleybus no. 61 (AHX 801) was also hired and demonstrated, using the wiring erected at The Level on 7th and 8th January 1936. This was the time of a town poll to gauge public opinion and to submit a Bill to Parliament in order for trolleybuses to run. The notice on the side states "The latest type of this trolleybus is free from wireless interference." Posters on the trolleybus and in Brighton Corporation's tram no. 69 urge people to "Vote for the Bill today." No. 61 was the only three-axle trolleybus to run in the town. (Lens of Sutton)

TRAMS TO TROLLEYBUSES

5. "THE OLD ORDER CHANGETH". So said the caption to this photograph, which appeared in the *Brighton and Hove Herald* on Saturday, 8th April 1939. No. 1, one of Brighton's new trolleybuses and running on Trade Plate 060 CD, is seen beside trams it would soon supersede at the western side of Old Steine in late afternoon sunshine. The official on the rear platform is giving the "thumbs up" signal, suggesting a successful day of testing. It made its first daylight tests on Monday, 3rd April 1939, possibly the day on which this photograph was taken.
(Brighton Herald Ltd)

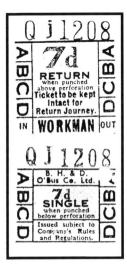

6. No. 1 is seen again, this time on Driver Training duties in April 1939 opposite the town's famous Royal Pavilion, built as a classical villa in 1786-7 by Henry Holland for the Prince Regent. It was enlarged in 1801-3 and between 1815 and 1822 was rebuilt in Indian style, designed by John Nash. (A.P.Henbest coll.)

7. Standing in the yard of Lewes Road Garage is one of the Corporation's AEC trolleybuses during the changeover from trams to trolleybuses. This photograph of brand new no. 5 seems likely to have been taken on the day of the official inauguration on 1st June 1939. Interestingly, the trams referred to this location as the Depot, but the trolleybuses displayed Garage. (The Omnibus Society)

8. With inaugural speeches made, Councillor Eric Simms drives the wonderfully decorated trolleybus no. 1 past the huge crowd at the Aquarium terminus and away on a tour of the routes to be converted to trolleybus operation later in the afternoon. On the platform is the Mayor of Brighton, Councillor J.Talbot Nanson, JP who has just pulled a lever to officially start the bus. The date is 1st June 1939 - a sunny day, but breezy judging by the flags. Note the white-walled tyres on no. 1 and the procession of brand-new trolleybuses, all devoid of advertisements, that were to start the services on routes 26 / 26A / 46 / 46A.
(Hamlin of Brighton)

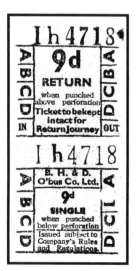

9. Temporary circular route 40 was introduced on 17th July 1939 when the trolleybus wires were extended from Brighton Station to Seven Dials. No. 36 is seen working in the clockwise direction using a second set of wires at the Aquarium terminus that had been strung by this time. The route lasted until services were revised following the final tramway abandonment on 31st August 1939. It was withdrawn with effect from 18th September 1939 as part of Wartime service reductions. (Crown)

BARRACKS, LEWES ROAD – LEWES ROAD GARAGE – ST PETER'S CHURCH – VICTORIA GARDENS – AQUARIUM, OLD STEINE

10. The first tram route in Brighton to be converted to trolleybuses was that along Lewes Road as this was the location of the Garage. From Monday, 1st May 1939, trolleybuses replaced trams between Aquarium, Old Steine and Lewes Road Barracks. There seems to be something of a fight to board no. 5, which is seen standing on the newly erected 72ft turning circle at the Barracks terminus, having arrived from the Aquarium. Some of its passengers are likely to be workers from the nearby Allen-West factory. Tramcars would have loaded on arrival here, but in trolleybus days, it was usual to turn first. It is possible that the conductor is advising those on the platform to board at the stop across the road. With intending passengers standing here and the attention that no. 5 has attracted from one of the girls and one of the gentlemen to its right, the photograph is likely to have been taken in the first few days of trolleybus operation in Brighton and possibly on the opening day. (A.P.Henbest coll.)

11. This view of Brighton Corporation's Transport Offices and Garage entrance, looking south-east, shows the wiring that allowed trolleybuses access north to the Barracks terminus in Lewes Road and south to the rest of the system. The building was constructed in just six months in 1901, originally to house Brighton's trams. The railway viaduct seen here carried the former Kemp Town branch line and was finally closed to freight traffic on 26th June 1971. All of the wiring shown here was retained to the end and was used for vehicle testing and driver training, although the Lewes Road route itself was abandoned in March 1959. Sadly by the time this photograph was taken on 30th July 1961, the trolleybuses had all gone. During May 2005, the offices to the south of the entrance were demolished to make way for a new transport office complex. (J.C.Gillham)

12. Inside Lewes Road Garage is a line-up of Brighton Corporation AEC trolleybuses. A 1959 Leyland PD2/37 is at the far end with other AEC buses. The liberal application of advertisements on Corporation vehicles meant that most could be identified from a distance. No. 30's destination blind is damaged and all of the trolleybooms are parked suggesting that these trolleybuses, including nos. 25, 38, 1 and 40, were awaiting their final trip to the breaker's yard. (A.P.Henbest coll.)

13. Travelling south and passing under the railway viaduct in Lewes Road (known locally as "The Arches") is Corporation BUT no. 50. The viaduct was demolished in 1978 to make way for a new road system and supermarket, but the pub just visible in the background survives. (W.J.Haynes / Southdown Enthusiasts Club)

14. No. 34 is seen heading north in Lewes Road, on the last afternoon of trolleybus operation in Brighton, 30th June 1961 by which time the nearside advertisement had been painted out. It was privately hired on the last evening, being replaced by no. 23. It was on its way back to the garage, out of service, to perform its last duty when this photograph was taken. The Lewes Road Inn on the left is now The Franklin Tavern. (London Trolleybus Preservation Society)

15. No. 12 is seen in Lewes Road at the bottom of Elm Grove having negotiated the frog that allowed trolleybuses to turn left and take up service on clockwise routes 41 / 42 or route 43A. The garage, like so many others in Lewes Road, is no longer in use for that purpose, but in 2005 is the Park Crescent New Surgery. St Martin's Church can be seen towering in the background. (Surfleet Negative Collection)

16. This view shows the bottom of Elm Grove during a power cut in 1948. It seems that both crews and passengers have left their vehicles, which suggests power has been off for some time. Both Corporation and Company trolleybuses are stranded – no. 6347 has only been in service for about eighteen months and is seen waiting to resume duties on summer only service 43 in front of no. 37. Smith's Radio became an Estate Agent. (Brighton Herald Ltd)

17. St Peter's Church, built of Portland Stone in the period 1824-8, has been the Parish Church of Brighton since 1873. It can be seen in the distance between the trees in this shot of no. 38, which is crossing the junction of Lewes Road with Union Road on 25th January 1958. The wires of routes 42 and 44 joined from the Open Market at this location. Many of the mature trees surrounding the local open space known as The Level were uprooted during the severe storm that hit the South of England in October 1987. Following replanting, the area is beginning to resemble its former glory. (Brighton Herald Ltd)

18. No. 37 is accelerating away from the traffic lights at St Peter's Church on its way south to the terminus at Old Steine. The tram shelter, which can be seen between the black and white poles, was moved to Amberley Working Museum, West Sussex and now acts as a passenger shelter for its railway. The concrete shelters have been replaced with a modern advertising shelter. (C.Carter)

19. It was a warm day when this pair of trolleybuses, nos 43 and 44, were photographed at the Grand Parade stop opposite Victoria Gardens. Before the trolleybuses finished, the stop was moved to the opposite side of the road with a traffic island for passengers to alight. It is now a bus lane and the Apex has become The Brighton Oasis – a sauna. (D.A.Jones)

20. Everyone except the two boys on the right is wearing coats in this view of the north end of Old Steine taken on the sunny afternoon of 1st June 1957. Standing outside J.Lyons' café (which is having a coat of paint) is Corporation trolleybus no. 9 on anticlockwise circular route 41. No. 5, with trolleybooms outstretched is approaching the "trolleybuses only" platform on route 46, closely followed by a Southdown Leyland single-decker bus. The wires diverged at the bracket arm where it appears a tower wagon is passing. The crossings associated with the links across the gardens can clearly be seen. (Brighton Herald Ltd)

21. Almost at the end of its journey is no. 30 in the lane reserved for "Trolley Buses only". The wiring emerging from St James's Street on the left has two more days' use – for the date is 22nd March 1959, the day the Norbury Transport and Model Railway Club toured the entire system using hired no. 1. On the extreme left is one of Southdown Motor Services Ltd's new Leyland PD3/4 buses with forward entrance bodywork working the town service 110 from Lower Bevendean to Old Steine. (J.C.Gillham)

22. No. 27 is seen leaving the penultimate stop on its way to the Aquarium, Old Steine terminus, with a Southdown Motor Services Ltd Leyland PD2/12 dating from 1955 behind. The latter is on route 18, which ran to Lewes, Heathfield and Hawkhurst jointly with Maidstone and District Motor Services Ltd. Partly visible to the left of the 1914-1918 War Memorial is one of Brighton, Hove and District's convertible open-top Bristol K5Gs. (W.J.Haynes / Southdown Enthusiasts Club)

23. Taken in August 1953 when the trolleybus fleet strength was at its maximum, this view shows a convoy of trolleybuses heading for their appropriate terminal loop of wiring. No. 46 in the foreground is staying on the inner set of wires as will the third trolleybus, no. 9, which shows short-working terminus Larkfield Way in its ultimate destination screen. The BUT behind no. 46 is about to take the frog for the outer set of wires and will negotiate another frog to gain the 48 terminus on the outermost loop. The AEC trolleybus at the rear will move to the outer set of wires here and then stay on the centre set of wires to reach its terminus. (R.F.Mack / C.W.Routh)

24. Ready for a journey to Hollingbury, no. 47 has yet to move to the loading island and is probably working a peak-hour extra service. Behind is 1948 Brighton, Hove and District Bristol K6B no. 386 (DNJ 995) on route 14, renumbered 54 in May 1961 as part of the B.A.T.S. agreement to avoid number clashes with the co-ordination of services. In the centre of the gardens is the Victoria Fountain, unveiled on 25th May 1846 to celebrate Queen Victoria's 27th birthday. The lower basin rests on the entwined figures of three dolphins – the coat-of-arms of the Borough of Brighton. Brighton's weather instruments are stored in the white box (a Stephenson Screen) standing on the grass. (W.J.Haynes / Southdown Enthusiasts Club)

25. As World War II drew to a close, trolleybuses began to appear in full red and cream livery with cream roofs. No. 6344 is operating on clockwise route 42 on this warm day, probably in the late spring or early summer of 1945. The two trolleybuses on its offside working to Preston Drove both still have grey roofs, while no. 6 behind is in all-over khaki livery. (The Omnibus Society)

26. Trolleybuses nos 26 and 20, with shining paintwork wait their departure times at the Aquarium, Old Steine terminus with masked headlights and white paint on their mudguards. Both have spotlights, they still have cream roofs and the tarmac shows where the tram tracks have been lifted. These things point to this photograph being taken early in wartime. Note the gentleman between the trolleybuses carrying a tin helmet. In 2005, Sam Isaac's restaurant is Harry Ramsden's restaurant. (J.Turley / DTP Library)

27. Even today, it would have to be something major to cause a traffic jam of the proportions seen here on 2nd October 1957. Ten trolleybuses are visible in amongst the interesting selection of cars, lorries and buses. In the centre of the photograph, carrying an advertisement for Vernon's Pools is Company trolleybus no. 6346 on route 42. Closer to the passenger shelter / staff rest room and third in line is one of the final BUT trolleybuses, no. 51 or 52. The other trolleybuses are all Corporation AECs. The Southdown Leyland PD2/12 dating from 1956 in the right foreground is on route 122 to Gravesend, operated jointly with Maidstone and District. Behind is a 1948 Southdown Leyland PD2/1 operating on route 113 introduced on 10th February 1957 to the rapidly expanding Woodingdean estate. By this time the fate of the trolleybuses had been sealed. (Evening Argus / DTP Library)

48	OLD STEINE — BARRACKS (Lewes Road)										48

Via Pavilion Parade, Gloucester Place, St. Peter's Church, Richmond Place, The Level, The Arches.

WEEKDAYS — WINTER (For period of operation see Page 1).

	a.m.	a.m.	a.m.	a.m.	a.m.	a.m.	a.m.		p.m.				
OLD STEINE	5 40	6 16	6 42	6 50	6 58	7 6	7 12	and every 5	11 2	......	......	......	......
BARRACKS	5 50	6 26	6 52	7 0	7 8	7 16	7 22	minutes until	1112	......	......	......	......

	a.m.	a.m.	a.m.	p.m.	a.m.	a.m.	a.m.		p.m.		
BARRACKS	5 3	5 20	6 5	6 31	6 39	6 47	6 55	7 1	and every 5	1051	* To Royal Pavilion only.
OLD STEINE	*	5 30	6 15	6 41	6 49	6 57	7 5	7 11	minutes until	11 1	

WEEKDAYS — MIDWINTER (For period of operation see Page 1).

	a.m.	a.m.	a.m.		p.m.	p.m.		p.m.	p.m.			
OLD STEINE	5 40	6 18	6 42	then every 6	7 6	7 13	then every 8	1057	11 5	......	......	......
BARRACKS	5 50	6 28	6 52	minutes until	7 16	7 23	minutes until	11 7	1115	......	......	......

	a.m.	a.m.	a.m.	a.m.	a.m.		p.m.	p.m.		p.m.	p.m.		
BARRACKS	5 2	5 20	5 30	6 7	6 31	then every 6	6 55	7 2	then every 8	1046	1054	......	......
OLD STEINE	5 12	5 30	5 40	6 17	6 41	minutes until	7 5	7 12	minutes until	1056	11 4	......	......

SUNDAYS — WINTER (For period of operation see Page 1). | **SUNDAYS — MIDWINTER** (For period of operation see Page 1).

	a.m.		p.m.				a.m. a.m.		p.m. p.m.
OLD STEINE	9 24	and every 6	11 0	......		OLD STEINE	9 13 9 21	then every 8	1057 11 5
BARRACKS	9 34	minutes until	1110	......		BARRACKS	9 23 9 31		11 7 1115

	a.m.		p.m.				a.m. a.m.		p.m. p.m.
BARRACKS	9 13	and every 6	1049	......		BARRACKS	9 29 10	then every 8	1046 1054
OLD STEINE	9 23	minutes until	1059	......		OLD STEINE	9 12 9 20	minutes until	1056 11 4

AQUARIUM, OLD STEINE – VICTORIA GARDENS –
ST PETER'S CHURCH – LONDON ROAD –
PRESTON CIRCUS

28. Four trolleybuses, including nos 1, 43 and 29 stand in the spring sunshine at the Aquarium, Old Steine terminus. The introduction of trolleybuses to Brighton brought an enormous improvement in street lighting to the roads they served using the type shown here.
(C.Bennett and M.Jenkins, Online Transport Archive)

→

29. The little boy standing at the 46 / 46A loading island at the Aquarium terminus seems oblivious to the driver using the bamboo pole to put no. 6341's trolleybooms on the wires before heading off to Brighton Races with his Race Special. Note the absence of the rear light next to the registration plate – on Company trolleybuses this was placed to the right of the "stopping" sign, below the circular advertisement for "Spratt's dog food". Notice also the flush rear destination box – another difference between the pre-war Company and Corporation trolleybuses.
(The Omnibus Society)

30. Corporation trolleybus no. 12 has left the Aquarium, Old Steine terminus and is heading for the Race Hill on regular service 43A in May 1951. On Race Days, crews were encouraged to leave their screens blank so that race-goers used the special services provided at a higher fare. Perhaps it is lunchtime - the Brighton Corporation Transport "Staff Canteen Service" Ford V8 Pilot van may have just made a delivery to the staff offices at the terminus. (A.B.Cross)

31. Parked on the west side of Old Steine is one of the Corporation AEC fleet which was decorated and used to encourage people to purchase War Savings Stamps. Throughout the war, there were national savings events to buy ships and planes to aid the war effort. "Brighton's Warship Week" ran from 7th – 14th February 1942. The notices in the trolleybus windows encourage people to "Step aboard and purchase your war savings stamps" and "certificates" with an advertisement for the Post Office Savings Bank between them. The "British bulldog" board attached to the front declares that "WAR SAVINGS are Warships…" Note the grey roof of the trolleybus, its white paint on the mudguards and the blacked out head and side lights. (A.P.Henbest coll.)

32. These two AEC trolleybuses, nos 38 and 35 will follow each other to Preston Drove, as there was no overtaking facility in the overhead wiring. The location is the Electricity Showrooms at the western end of Old Steine and it is late morning on 18th September 1960 as the couple cross the road with virtually no traffic to worry about. Today this crossing is controlled by sets of lights and there is far more traffic. Just past the traffic lights today is a contra-flow bus lane while the Royal Bank of Scotland occupies the former Electricity Showrooms building. (C.Horlock coll.)

33. The inscription on the North Gate of the Royal Pavilion reads WR IIII AD MDCCCXXXII, meaning it was erected during the reign of King William IV in 1832. Corporation trolleybus no. 6 is seen passing some time in the period 1949-1951 after route 46 had been extended to Hollingbury, but before it was diverted to run via Surrenden Road, Braybon Avenue and Carden Avenue. (C.Horlock coll.)

34. Also passing the Royal Pavilion is a Corporation AEC trolleybus. The bronze statue of George IV by Sir Francis Chantrey was erected in 1828 at the cost of 3,000 guineas, collected by public subscription. The photograph dates from shortly after the tram service finished and clearly shows the link wiring from Grand Parade to Marlborough Place on bracket arm suspension. (E.F.Bristoll coll.)

35. This early morning view shows no. 23 followed by no. 35 in Marlborough Place, with North Gate House in the background. The sunlight accentuates the lines of the buildings. Just a few yards out of shot to the right is the famous "King and Queen" public house, partly visible in the right background of the next view. (M.P.M.Nimmo)

36. No. 38 crosses from Marlborough Place to Gloucester Place with two Corporation AEC motorbuses in the background. Victoria Gardens and fountain are behind the trees and the olive green Post Office Telephones' Morris Minor. Anticlockwise route 42 would have crossed from right to left at this point, prior to March 1959. (F.W.Ivey)

37. With the buildings of St George's Place and Gloucester Place in the background, Corporation BUT no. 51 has selected the wires that will take it onto Lewes Road. Those behind it attached to the bracket arm continue to London Road. (Surfleet Negative Collection)

38. A Corporation AEC trolleybus heads northwards on the A23 trunk road, Brighton's second shopping street, on a sunny afternoon amid assorted 1950s traffic. The wiring in London Road is suspended from bracket arms, span wires attached to traction poles and span wires attached to rosettes, as on the Co-op building in the centre left of the photograph. The Co-op with its rosettes is still there today, as are most of the buildings seen here. The trolleybus will shut off power to pass under the positive and negative feeders. 690 yards (631 metres) of London Road, including the section shown here, carried overhead wires for the 1913-14 trolleybus trials. (Brighton History Centre, Brighton and Hove City Council)

39. At the end of London Road, no. 42 is about to turn into Beaconsfield Road at the Preston Circus roundabout in this late afternoon view. The east-west wires of former routes 42 and 44 have been removed showing that the photograph was taken after March 1959. A twin-line hanger that once carried wires for a left turn into New England Road remains. Routes 40A and "inner circle" route 40 used this wiring until they were withdrawn as a result of expansion of the system and wartime reductions respectively. The "Hare and Hounds" public house, dating from 1905, in the centre of the picture, survives. (London Trolleybus Preservation Society)

40. This photograph was taken looking north in London Road towards the complex trolleybus junction at Preston Circus on 30th June 1956. The wiring allowing a left turn into New England Road can be seen, but the connection from New England Road to London Road, was dismantled in the mid-1950s. The wiring leading to the roundabout and into Beaconsfield Road was used from 1st June 1939 until the end of the system for routes 46 and 46A. Wiring can also be seen running from west to east across Preston Circus for use by "outer circle" route 42 and route 44 from 1st September 1939 until they were withdrawn at the first stage of the conversion programme. The trolleybus in the right distance is about to pass under the viaduct which carries the railway to Lewes, Eastbourne and Hastings in the east. Geary's Furniture shop is now Ashton's, while The Stanford Arms in the centre has been renamed Circus Circus. (Brighton Herald Ltd)

VICTORIA GARDENS – NORTH ROAD – BRIGHTON STATION – SEVEN DIALS

41. Brighton, Hove and District trolleybus no. 346 is seen at the bottom of North Road on anticlockwise route 42. It will cross into Grand Parade and continue to its terminal point outside J.Lyons café at the east side of Old Steine. It was usual to change to "inner circle" route 41 at the café, hence the temporarily incorrect blind display. Redhill Motors' building has recently been refurbished and extended to form new restaurant-bar premises. (P.D.Williams coll.)

42 CLOCK-WISE	CIRCULAR **OLD STEINE — BRIGHTON STATION — QUEEN'S PARK ROAD — OLD STEINE** Via Pavilion Parade, North Road, Queens Road, Brighton Station, Seven Dials, Preston Circus, Viaduct Road, The Level, Elm Grove, Queen's Park Road, Egremont Place, Rock Gardens, St. James's Street.	**42** CLOCK-WISE

WEEKDAYS — WINTER (For period of operation see Page 1).

	a.m.	a.m.	a.m.	a.m.		a.m.	a.m.	a.m.	a.m.	a.m.	a.m.	a.m.	a.m.	a.m.	a.m.			p.m.
OLD STEINE	......	5 48	6 18	......		6 46	6 56	7 6	7 18	7 30	7 42	7 54	8	8 13				6 53
BRIGHTON STATION (arr.)	......	5 54	6 24	......		6 52	7	7 12	7 24	7 36	7 48	8 0	8 7	8 19				6 59
BRIGHTON STATION (dep.)	......	5 57	6 25	......		6 52	7 3	7 15	7 27	7 39	7 51	8 2	8 12	8 22		Then every		6 59
SEVEN DIALS	......	6 0	6 28	6 38	6 48	6 55	7 6	7 18	7 30	7 42	7 54	8 5	8 15	8 25		10 minutes		7 2
PRESTON CIRCUS	......	6 2	6 30	6 40	6 52	6 59	7 10	7 22	7 34	7 46	7 58	8 9	8 19	8 29		until		7 7
OPEN MARKET	......	6 4	6 32	6 42	6 52	6 59	7 10	7 22	7 34	7 46	7 58	8 9	8 19	8 29				7 7
QUEEN'S PARK JUNCTION	5 40	6 10	6 38	6 47	6 57	7 4	7 16	7 28	7 40	7 52	8 4	8 15	8 25	8 35				7 15
OLD STEINE	5 48	6 18	6 46	6 55	7 5	7 12	7 24	7 36	7 48	8 0	8 12	8 23	8 33	8 43				7 23

											p.m.			
OLD STEINE				6	18	30	42	54			1054			
BRIGHTON STATION (arr.)				12	24	36	48	0			11 0	......	......	......
BRIGHTON STATION (dep.)		Then at		15	27	39	51	3			11 5	......	......	......
SEVEN DIALS		these minutes		18	30	42	54	6	until		11 8	......	......	......
PRESTON CIRCUS		past each hour		21	33	45	57	9			1111	......	......	......
OPEN MARKET				23	35	47	59	11			1113	......	......	......
QUEEN'S PARK JUNCTION				28	40	52	4	16			1118	......	......	......
OLD STEINE				36	48	0	12	24			1126	......	......	......

WEEKDAYS — MIDWINTER (For period of operation see Page 1).

	a.m.	a.m.	a.m.	a.m.	a.m.	a.m.	a.m.								p.m.
OLD STEINE	......	5 48	6 18	......	6 46	6 56	7 6		6	18	30	42	54		1054	......	......
BRIGHTON STATION (arr.)	......	5 54	6 24	......	6 52	7	7 12		12	24	36	48	0		11 0	......	......
BRIGHTON STATION (dep.)	......	5 57	6 25	......	6 52	7 3	7 15	Then at	15	27	39	51	3		11 5	......	......
SEVEN DIALS	......	6 0	6 28	6 38	6 48	6 55	7 6	these minutes	18	30	42	54	6	until	11 8	......	......
PRESTON CIRCUS	......	6 2	6 30	6 40	6 50	6 57	8 7	past each hour	21	33	45	57	9		1111	......	......
OPEN MARKET	......	6 4	6 32	6 42	6 52	6 59	7 7		23	35	47	59	11		1113	......	......
QUEEN'S PARK JUNCTION	5 40	6 10	6 38	6 47	6 57	7 7	7 16		28	40	52	4	16		1118	......	......
OLD STEINE	5 48	6 18	6 46	6 55	7 5	7 12	7 24		36	48	0	12	24		1126	......	......

42. At the top of North Road, no. 6 is seen passing Brighton's postal Sorting Office and is about to turn right into Queen's Road on its way to Brighton Station. The trolleybus overhead was mostly carried on bracket arms in this narrow road. (P.D.Williams coll.)

43. Corporation trolleybus no. 48 is parked on the little used wiring in Surrey Street when on hire to the Southern Counties Touring Society for a tour of the system in 1958. Race Specials would have used the wiring and turned right here into Brighton Station, as would trolleybuses working peak summer route 40B from the Aquarium, Old Steine to Brighton Station via North Road. The straight-ahead wiring was used to gain access to Seven Dials without the need for de- and re-poling service vehicles on clockwise route 42. (D.A.Jones / London Trolleybus Preservation Society)

44. The Brighton station terminal area has been remodelled in recent years, but here Corporation trolleybus no. 40 stands at the loading platform for anticlockwise route 42 alongside a Bristol KSW6B belonging to the Company dating from 1952. The extension of route 6 to Southwick station started on 25th February 1957, dating this photograph to within two years. Note the white steering wheel on the Bristol, which was used to indicate an eight-foot wide body. (C.Carter)

45. The overhead junction used for Race Specials to reverse right up to Brighton station's entrance can clearly be seen as lightly loaded Company no. 6345 leaves for a trip to the Aquarium. Today the five-storey International House has replaced the hoardings and Hudson's building, seen in the following picture. (Photobus)

46. The driver of Brighton, Hove and District trolleybus no. 346 is releasing the hand brake to leave Brighton station and head off for the Seven Dials in the 1950s. Following is 1947 Brighton Corporation AEC Regent III no. 83 (HUF 83), while parked at its terminal stand and facing in the opposite direction is a BH&D Bristol KSW6B dating from 1951 / 2. Behind the Corporation bus, the tower wagon can just be seen. (Surfleet Negative coll.)

47. Nearing the end of its career, no. 342 has turned at the Seven Dials from Chatham Place into Buckingham Place on its way to Brighton Station. The bus that has passed in the opposite direction was one of the last rear entrance Leyland PD 2/12s bought by Southdown which featured a sliding platform door. The Seven Dials roundabout is much smaller in 2005, both banks seen in this view have closed and this part of Buckingham Place is a one-way street. (R. Ticehurst coll.)

SEVEN DIALS – PRESTON CIRCUS –
OPEN MARKET – UNION ROAD

48. Company no. 6391 is captured on the roundabout at Seven Dials having negotiated a facing frog, a crossing and a trailing frog, which must have required considerable skill on the part of the driver at this busy intersection. Also on the roundabout is a Brighton "Streamline" taxi with its distinctive cream bonnet – the Company bus behind the trolleybus in Buckingham Place is on the 7 group of routes heading for Brighton Station. In the distance is Brighton's incinerator chimney, demolished in the 1960s and replaced with two tower blocks of flats.
(W.J.Haynes / Southdown Enthusiasts Club)

49. The same vehicle has just arrived at Seven Dials from Black Rock and is seen on a summer evening at the terminal stop in Chatham Place. The driver appears to be returning to his seat having changed the ultimate destination blind for the return journey on this busy service. Passengers were not carried around the terminal loop. (A.B.Cross)

50. The railway bridge framing no. 6344 carries the main line from Brighton to London and also that to Lewes, Eastbourne and Hastings. The trolleybus has come from the Seven Dials terminus and is on the main east to west A27 trunk road through Brighton and Hove, which joined New England Road in the "tunnel". The usual procedure was to switch the internal lights on when entering, and off when leaving the "tunnel". The Gents' toilet, behind the man who is waving to someone on the trolleybus, has long been demolished; the advertising hoardings have been removed and the walls since graffitied. (F.W. Ivey)

SUNDAYS — WINTER AND MIDWINTER (For period of operation see Page i).

	a.m.	a.m.								p.m.					
OLD STEINE		9 18			6	18	30	42	54	1054					
BRIGHTON STATION (arr)		9 24			12	24	36	48	0	11 0					
BRIGHTON STATION (dep.)		9 27	and at these		15	27	39	51	3	11 5					
SEVEN DIALS		9 30	minutes past		18	30	42	54	6	until	11 8				
PRESTON CIRCUS		9 33	each hour		21	33	45	57	9	1111					
OPEN MARKET		9 35			23	35	47	59	11	1113					
QUEEN'S PARK JUNCTION	9 10	9 40			28	40	52	4	16	1118					
OLD STEINE	9 18	9 48			36	48	0	12	24	1126					

51. A little further down New England Road, BH&D trolleybus no. 6343 is seen on its way to Preston Circus, passing under the railway bridge that formerly carried trains to Brighton's Goods station. The bus ascending the hill is almost certainly a Bristol KSW6G used on route 38 which was intended to be a trolleybus service. (F.W.Ivey)

52. Heading west and crossing an empty Preston Circus is Corporation no. 1 on 1st February 1959. Viaduct Road in the background is now an east bound, one-way street that carries A23 traffic to Brighton seafront. Brighton Fire Station is still in use today as the Divisional Headquarters and carries the wall rosettes formerly used to support the overhead wiring. (E.F.Bristoll coll.)

53. Company no. 6345 is about to leave the almost empty A27 and turn right towards the Open Market. Between the rear of the trolleybus and the Guinness advertisement is one of a small number of pre-fab houses that were erected here. The overhead wiring is suspended unusually from "adjustable-leg" twin line hangers with porcelain insulators and tubular steel spacer bars. The distant skyline today is dominated by an office block built in the 1960s. (W.J.Haynes / Southdown Enthusiasts Club)

54. With the Royal Engineers Record Office as a backdrop, lightly loaded no. 6345 has an incorrect ultimate destination screen as it turns out of Viaduct Road into Ditchling Road, briefly joining the wires of routes 26 / 26A. The Grade II listed building is now occupied by The Brighton Business Centre. (Southdown Enthusiasts Club)

55. The Salvation Army Hall, replaced in 2003 with a modern building, is seen behind Company no. 6344, sporting circular mirrors as it leaves the loading island of Union Road and negotiates the roundabout at the Open Market on its way to Seven Dials. (Southdown Enthusiasts Club)

ELM GROVE – QUEEN'S PARK ROAD – ST JAMES' STREET – AQUARIUM, OLD STEINE

56. The mother and daughter on the right of the photograph appear to be posing in this winter view of the bottom of Elm Grove. The bus stop at this location was moved to a more inconvenient position for passengers in the mid-1960s when it was policy to build bus lay-bys. No. 21 glides down to the junction with Lewes Road, leaving another Corporation AEC to load and follow. St Joseph's Roman Catholic Church is in the background. (Surfleet Negative coll.)

57. About two-thirds of the way up Elm Grove, the trolleybus wires split - one branch continued the length of the hill to the Racecourse while the other turned into Queen's Park Road where Corporation no. 36 is seen before continuing into Elm Grove on 8th March 1959. Trolleybuses ran every ten minutes on each of the routes 41 and 42 and also every ten minutes on routes 43A and 44 serving the Race Hill, giving an intensive service on the lower part of Elm Grove. The coasting brake would have been applied at this stop to descend Elm Grove, which has a maximum gradient of 1 in 12. (L.W.Rowe)

58. On the opposite side of Queen's Park Road is Company no. 6345 loading in the afternoon sunshine on "Outer Circle" route 42. AEC trolleybuses could come to grief at the junction with Elm Grove if a more powerful BUT trolleybus was following close behind as the latter tended to drain the current. The electric frog was set in favour of the Queen's Park Road routes, but if the driver of an AEC had to apply power to proceed up Elm Grove at the activator, the wrong wires could be taken with potentially disastrous results. (W.J.Haynes / Southdown Enthusiasts Club)

59. Speeding along Queen's Park Road at the junction with Pankhurst Avenue and Down Terrace is Company no. 6347. Deep under the Chalk is the tunnel for the Kemp Town branch railway, which followed the line of Carlyle Street opposite. (W.J.Haynes / Southdown Enthusiasts Club)

60. This sunny mid-day shot shows Company no. 343 turning into St James's Street from Upper Rock Gardens on clockwise route 41. This was the tram terminus for the routes to Seven Dials and Old Steine via Queen's Park Road and Elm Grove. The link to Old Steine allowing circular services to operate was one of the trolleybus extensions beyond the tram system. The Corporation AEC trolleybus on anticlockwise route 41 in the background is absorbing some of the people in the queue but a lot are waiting for other motorbus services that served this bus stop. (M.Dryhurst)

61. In trolleybus days St James's Street (on the destination blind referred to here as St. James St) was a two-way thoroughfare and a thriving shopping street. Corporation no. 11 has turned the corner at J.Lyons' Café from Old Steine and is making its way up the incline on a wet day in the mid-1950s. Today, St. James's Street is a one-way street in the direction the trolleybus is travelling. (By kind permission of the Royal Pavilion Libraries and Museums, Brighton and Hove, 2005)

62. Corporation no. 4 is turning into Old Steine at the bottom of a busy St James's Street. The splicing in the overhead shows where the wiring continued both ways across the gardens to the western side of Old Steine until at least June 1957. The section insulator box outside Maynards, where the paper seller is sitting, remained for many years after the trolleybuses finished. (C.Carter)

PRESTON DROVE

26
A

St PETERS CH
OPEN MARKET
DITCHLING Rᴰ

22 CHURCH

26

FUF 26

63. The Aquarium, Old Steine was the terminus for almost all of Brighton's trolleybus routes. Here Corporation no. 26 and Company no. 6393 have arrived and stand side by side in 1951 when

RACE HILL
43A THE LEVEL
ELM GROVE

DNJ 994

there were only two sets of wires. The subtle differences between the pre-war AEC on the left and the post-war BUT on the right can be seen. (A.B.Cross)

ELM GROVE – RACE HILL – MANOR HILL –
WHITEHAWK GARAGE –
BLACK ROCK

64. "Applejohn's Cider Bar" is advertised by Corporation no. 31 which has arrived at the Race Hill terminus of route 43A at the top of Elm Grove. After the trolleybuses finished, I used to change buses here when travelling to and from secondary school and missed the warmth of the tram shelter when it was replaced with "modern" facilities. On a clear day, the Isle of Wight can be seen rising out of the English Channel from here, a distance of some fifty miles. (C.Carter)

65. At the Race Hill a Company AEC is stranded on the turning circle in the late afternoon - possibly near the end of a Race Day, as there are plenty of people about. The trolleybus has probably hit the kerb and has de-wired when reversing, with the trolleybooms becoming suck in the overhead. The crew have leant the bamboo pole against the vehicle and seem to be otherwise engaged while waiting for a tow. The shadows suggest that there is another vehicle waiting to turn behind the trolleybus. The policeman, wearing his distinctive white helmet, is allowing people across the road to the trolleybuses and motorbuses that would be waiting to the left of the cameraman to take them back to Brighton Station or to the Aquarium. Notice that there are a good number of coaches and cars parked in the field in the distance opposite the racecourse. There was talk of Brighton Town Council spending an estimated £40,000 on extending the trolleybus system over two miles from here to the growing suburb of Woodingdean beyond the racecourse in the mid-1950s. (J.Turley / DTP Library)

43a   **OLD STEINE   —   RACE HILL**   **43a**

Via Pavilion Parade, Gloucester Place, St. Peter's Church, Richmond Place, The Level, Elm Grove.

WEEKDAYS — WINTER (For period of operation see Page 1).

WEEKDAYS — MIDWINTER (For period of operation see Page 1).

SUNDAYS — WINTER AND MIDWINTER (For period of operation see Page 1).

TENDER THE CORRECT FARE — STATE YOUR DESTINATION

66. This view of Corporation no. 6 was taken on 8th March 1959, just before route 43A was withdrawn at the first stage of the conversion programme. The crew have left the trolleybus to either visit the toilet (now a café), partly obscured by the vehicle itself, or crossed the road to have a cup of tea at the Downs Café, or both! Some of the racecourse buildings can be seen behind the trolleybus on the hill. (L.W.Rowe)

67. Company no. 344 was a regular performer on the 44 route as these next views show. On a cold winter's day, it has turned into icy Freshfield Road carrying a full load. Note the light indicator strapped to the traction pole to show in which direction the frog was set. The fencing on the brow of the hill shows where the racecourse is. Today the area seems less bleak, as there are more fences and buildings. A Garden Centre has now been built on the slope to the right of the trolleybus. (John Fozard / Bob Mack coll.)

Via New England Road, Preston Circus, Viaduct Road, The Level, Elm Grove, Race Hill, Manor Hill, Whitehawk Road, Arundel Road.

WEEKDAYS — WINTER (For period of operation see Page 1).

	a.m. a.m. a.m. a.m. a.m. a.m.		p.m. p.m.				p.m.
SEVEN DIALS	6 15 7 13 7 25 7 37 7 49 8 0	and then every	7 0 7 13	and at these	1 13 25 37 49		1049 ......
RACE HILL	6 26 7 24 7 36 7 48 8 0 8 11	10 minutes	7 11 7 24	minutes past	12 24 36 48 0	until	11 0 ......
BLACK ROCK	7 33 7 45 7 57 8 9 8 20	until	7 20 7 33	each hour	21 33 45 57 9		11 9 ......

	a.m. a.m. a.m. a.m. a.m. a.m.		p.m. p.m.				p.m.
BLACK ROCK	6 52 7 4 7 16 7 28 7 40	and then every	6 40 6 52	and at these	4 16 28 40 52		1028 ......
RACE HILL	7 1 7 13 7 25 7 37 7 49	10 minutes	6 49 7 1	minutes past	13 25 37 49 1	until	1037 ......
SEVEN DIALS	7 12 7 24 7 36 7 48 8 0	until	7 0 7 12	each hour	24 36 48 0 12		1048 ......

WEEKDAYS — MIDWINTER (For period of operation see Page 1).

	a.m.						p.m.					p.m. p.m.
SEVEN DIALS	7 13	Then at these	25 37 49 1 13		until	7 25	Then at these	40 55 10 25		until	1040 1051 ... ..
RACE HILL	7 24	minutes	36 48 0 12 24			7 36	minutes	51 6 21 36			1051 11 2 ......
BLACK ROCK	7 33	past each hour	45 57 9 21 33			7 45	past each hour	0 15 30 45			11 0 11 11 ......

	a.m.					p.m. p.m.					p.m. p.m.
BLACK ROCK	6 52	Then at these	4 16 28 40 52	until	7 4 7 19	Then at these	34 49 4 19	until	1019 1031
RACE HILL	7 1	minutes	13 25 37 49 1		7 13 7 28	minutes	43 58 13 28		1028 1040
SEVEN DIALS	7 12	past each hour	24 36 48 0 12		7 24 7 39	past each hour	54 9 24 39		1039 1050

SUNDAYS — WINTER (For period of operation see Page 1).

	a.m.			p.m.
SEVEN DIALS	9 25	and at these	1 13 25 37 49	1049
RACE HILL	9 36	mins. past	12 24 36 48 0	11 0
BLACK ROCK	9 45	each hour	21 33 45 57 9	11 9

	a.m.				p.m.
BLACK ROCK	9 5	and at these	5 17 29 41 53		1029
RACE HILL	9 14	mins. past	14 26 38 50 2	until	1038
SEVEN DIALS	9 25	each hour	25 37 49 1 13		1049

SUNDAYS — MIDWINTER (For period of operation see Page 1).

	a.m.				p.m.
SEVEN DIALS	9 30	Then at these	45 0 15 30		1045
RACE HILL	9 41	minutes	56 11 26 41	until	1056
BLACK ROCK	9 50	past each hour	5 20 35 50		11 5

	a.m.				p.m.
BLACK ROCK	9 9	Then at these	24 39 54 9		1024
RACE HILL	9 18	minutes	33 48 3 18	until	1033
SEVEN DIALS	9 29	past each hour	44 59 14 29		1044

68. No. 344 is seen passing the Grandstand of Brighton Racecourse further on in Freshfield Road, having climbed up from the Race Hill terminus of route 43A. It will slow to make the tight left turn into Manor Hill just past the cameraman. The tall traction poles, which additionally carried street lighting on the trolleybus routes, can clearly be seen. (F.W.Ivey)

69. The same vehicle has turned from Freshfield Road into Manor Hill in this icy view taken in March 1955 when it carried fleet no. 6344 and circular mirrors. Some of Brighton Racecourse stables are on the extreme right of the picture. Today, the bus shelter has disappeared, while a mini roundabout has appeared at the junction behind the trolleybus. (C.W.Routh coll.)

70. Also seen in Manor Hill, high above Brighton town centre, is Company BUT no. 393, which has just crossed the Racecourse. On Race Days, the road was closed here and trolleybuses on route 44 from Seven Dials made a battery turn at the curve shown in the previous photograph. One trolleybus also provided a shuttle service from Black Rock to this point, reversing using its batteries onto rough ground. (K.Lane coll.)

71. A Company AEC trolleybus on route 44 weaves its way towards Black Rock around the tight curves of Manor Way and into Whitehawk Crescent. The route was opened to trolleybuses on 3rd March 1946 to serve the growing Whitehawk estate on the eastern side of the town. This photograph was taken shortly after the route opened as the vehicle still carries its original hubcaps. (P.D.Williams coll.)

72. Emerging from Brighton, Hove and District's Whitehawk Garage is no. 345. It is on its way to work an afternoon peak-hour extra on route 26, which was normally operated by Corporation vehicles. (F.W.Ivey)

73. Showing blinds for route 43, which worked regularly on Summer Sundays until 1950, no. 347 is seen posed inside Whitehawk Garage on 22nd March 1959. Two other AEC trolleybuses are also parked in the garage. The cream and black open-top Bristol K5Gs will need to have their dust covers removed and be prepared for Easter service as Good Friday was on 27th March 1959. (F.W.Ivey)

74. Possibly the only time a Corporation trolleybus passed through the Company Garage was on Sunday, 22nd March 1959 during the three-hour tour of the system using no.1, organised by Gerry Daniels for the Norbury Transport and Model Railway Club. No. 344 has a flush front destination box, but no front hubcaps nor the borough coat-of-arms under the fleet name – three of the differences between the Company and Corporation AEC trolleybuses. (F.W.Ivey)

75. On 8th March 1959, no. 344 stands outside Whitehawk Road's Co-op supermarket. The notice in the Co-op's window states "this is a self service shop", whereas there is probably a notice in the trolleybus's near side window stating that trolleybuses are about to be replaced. (L.W.Rowe)

→
76. The only significant incident involving a Company trolleybus occurred on 7th February 1957. AEC no. 347 caught fire when climbing Elm Grove fully loaded on route 44 during the afternoon rush hour. The resistors overheating caused the fire, but damage was confined to the immediate electrical equipment. Following overhaul at Conway Street and modification of the front air ventilators, no. 347 returned to service and is seen here in its new guise outside St Mark's School in Arundel Road. (Surfleet Negative coll.)

→
77. Seen on the opposite side of the road at the north end of Arundel Road is Company no. 342. St Mark's School is behind the fencing on the left, but today, this has been demolished and replaced with the Bell Tower Industrial Estate. (Surfleet Negative coll.)

78. The uncollected fare box can be seen on the rear platform of no. 6340 which has turned off the seafront into Arundel Street behind sister Company AEC trolleybus no. 6344 on 23rd March 1951. The hook of the bamboo pole stored underneath no. 6340 can also be seen. Both trolleybuses have a simplified "via" screen with three lines of information. In the background is the French Convalescent Home, built in 1898, which is now The French Apartments. (J.H.Meredith)

79. Having left the Black Rock terminus of route 44, Company no. 392 is now in De Courcel Road and about to re-join Arundel Road at the end of the one-way anticlockwise loop. There is evidence that no. 392 at some time had carried a nearside fog lamp. In the background is the cutting carrying the A259 road to Rottingdean, Newhaven, Seaford, Eastbourne, Hastings and beyond. The view is partly blocked today by a seven-storey block of flats. (Surfleet Negative coll.)

PRESTON CIRCUS – BEACONSFIELD ROAD – BEACONSFIELD VILLAS – PRESTON DROVE

80. Passing the Stanford Arms at Preston Circus, Corporation no. 42 leaves Beaconsfield Road and heads for the London Road shops. Part of the railway viaduct can be seen above the trees in the distance. This photograph was taken late in trolleybus days, for the wires of routes 42 and 44 which crossed here, have been removed. About to follow the trolleybus is Southdown 524 (PUF 624), a Guy Arab IV dating from 1956 which has arrived at Preston Circus on the hourly service from Hassocks, Haywards Heath and Crawley. (Surfleet Negative coll.)

Via Royal Pavilion, Grand Parade, Victoria Gardens, London Road, Preston Circus, Beaconsfield Road, Beaconsfield Villas, Preston Drove, *Fiveways, Ditchling Road, The Level, Victoria Gardens, Grand Parade, Royal Pavilion.*

WEEKDAYS — WINTER (For periods of operation see Page I).

		a.m. a.m. a.m.		p.m. p.m.			p.m.	
OLD STEINE	dep.	5 55 6 6 25	then every	7 8 7 13	then at these	19 25 31 37 43 49 55 1 7 13	1031	THEN AS
BEACONSFIELD VILLAS	,,	6 7 6 18 6 37	7 minutes	7 20 7 25	minutes past	31 37 43 49 55 1 7 13 19 25 until	1043	SUNDAYS
FIVEWAYS	,,	6 9 6 20 6 39	until	7 22 7 27	each hour	33 39 45 51 57 3 9 15 21 27	1045	WINTER
OLD STEINE	arr.	6 20 6 31 6 50		7 33 7 38		44 50 56 2 8 14 20 26 32 38	1056	

WEEKDAYS — MIDWINTER (For period of operation see Page I).

		a.m. a.m. a.m.		p.m. p.m.					p.m. p.m. p.m.	
OLD STEINE	dep.	5 55 6 6 25	then every	7 8 7 20	then at these	32	44	56	8	20	1032 1044 1056	† To Lewes
BEACONSFIELD VILLAS	,,	6 7 6 18 6 37	7 minutes	7 20 7 32	minutes past	44	56	8	20	32 until	1044 1056 1 8	Garage
FIVEWAYS	,,	6 9 6 20 6 39	until	7 22 7 38	each hour	50	2	14	26	38	1050 1058 1110	
OLD STEINE	arr.	6 20 6 31 6 50		7 33 7 49		1	13	25	37	49	11 1 † †	

SUNDAYS — WINTER (For period of operation see Page I).

		a.m.				p.m. p.m. p.m. p.m. p.m. p.m.	
OLD STEINE	dep.	9 13	then at these	19 25 31 37 43 49 55 1 7 13		1031 1037 1043 1049 1055 11 1	† To Lewes Road
BEACONSFIELD VILLAS	,,	9 25	minutes	31 37 43 49 55 1 7 13 19 25 until		1043 1049 1055 11 1 11 7 1113	Garage
FIVEWAYS	,,	9 27	past each	33 39 45 51 57 3 9 15 21 27		1045 1051 1057 11 3 11 9 1115	
OLD STEINE	arr.	9 38	hour	44 50 56 2 8 14 20 26 32 38		1056 † † † † †	

SUNDAYS — MIDWINTER (For period of operation see Page I).

		a.m.							p.m. p.m. p.m. p.m. p.m.	
OLD STEINE	dep.	9 8	then at these	20	32	44	56	8	1020 1032 1044 1056 11 1	† To Lewes
BEACONSFIELD VILLAS	,,	9 20	minutes	32	44	56	8	20 until	1032 1044 1056 11 8 1113	Road Garage
FIVEWAYS	,,	9 26	past each	38	50	2	14	26	1038 1046 1058 1110 1115	
OLD STEINE	arr.	9 37	hour	49	1	13	25	37	1049 1057 † † †	

81. During the last days of Brighton trolleybuses, no. 27 is seen heading south towards Preston Circus about to pass under the railway viaduct in Beaconsfield Road when traffic flowed in both directions. Today, Beaconsfield Road is one-way southbound and part of the A23 Trunk Road into Brighton city centre. (London Trolleybus Preservation Society)

82. Carrying a capacity load of workers from the Hollingbury Industrial Estate, no. 23 crosses from Beaconsfield Villas to Beaconsfield Road at Stanford Avenue, which leads up to Fiveways. The photograph can be dated to 1952, for no. 23 is carrying black pennants on its trolleybooms to mourn the death of King George VI on 6th February. (A.P.Henbest coll.)

83. In the 1950s, a roundabout was built at the junction of Stanford Avenue, Beaconsfield Villas, Beaconsfield Road and Florence Road. The trolleybus wiring was altered and no. 10 is about to negotiate it when the roundabout was new. Beaconsfield Villas can be seen stretching into the distance where another Corporation trolleybus can just be discerned. (Brighton Herald Ltd)

PRESTON DROVE – FIVEWAYS –
DITCHLING ROAD – OPEN MARKET –
ST PETER'S CHURCH

84. The man with the walking stick and the mother pushing a period pushchair only have to watch out for Corporation no. 24, when crossing Beaconsfield Villas, as the trolleybus passes under the crossing and begins to ascend Preston Drove. The driver and conductor have already turned the blinds for the return journey into town. (C.Carter)

85. The photographer is standing on a traffic island at Fiveways and is looking west along Preston Drove at two Corporation AEC trolleybuses. No. 15 will wait for a few minutes before returning to the Aquarium via Ditchling Road, while no. 38 will wait further down the road before returning to the same terminus via Beaconsfield Villas. No. 38's conductor has wound the rear blind round for the return journey. Both are about to pass under the positive and negative feeders and both sport newly painted advertisements for "Fremlin's beers". The trolleybuses have only a few months to run, as the date is 4th September 1960. (A.D.Packer)

86. No. 1 passes under the crossing in the overhead as it pulls out of Preston Drove and into Ditchling Road for the downhill journey into town. The roads seem clean and relatively free of traffic at this busy location. The Co-op at Fiveways, seen behind the Morris car on this warm day, is still trading in 2005, while the junction is now controlled by traffic lights. The 'tween decks advertisement panel has been blanked out ready for a signwriter to paint an updated advertisement for "Littlewoods Pools". (D.A.Thompson)

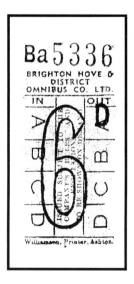

Ba5336
BRIGHTON HOVE &
DISTRICT
OMNIBUS CO. LTD.
IN   OUT
A   D
B   C
C   B
D   C
6
Williamson, Printer, Ashton.

87. It is a sunny, spring afternoon and Brighton Corporation no. 4 is seen loading at The Downs School stop on its way into Brighton. In 2005, the junction with Upper Hollingdean Road, which is behind and to the right of the trolleybus, is controlled by traffic lights. The school and the tram shelter remain. (J.Bishop)

26a / 46a OLD STEINE — FIVEWAYS — BEACONSFIELD VILLAS — OLD STEINE 26a / 46a

Via Royal Pavilion, Grand Parade, Victoria Gardens, The Level, Ditchling Road, Fiveways, *Preston Drove, Beaconsfield Villas, Beaconsfield Road, Preston Circus, London Road, Victoria Gardens, Grand Parade, Royal Pavilion.*

WEEKDAYS — WINTER (For period of operation see Page 1).

	a.m.	a.m.		p.m.	p.m.														p.m.	p.m.
OLD STEINE	6 3	6 22	then every	7 5	7 16	then at these	22	28	34	40	46	52	58	4	10	16		1058	11 8
FIVEWAYS	6 14	6 33	7 minutes	7 16	7 27	minutes past	33	39	45	51	57	3	9	15	21	27		11 9	1119
BEACONSFIELD VILLAS	6 16	6 35	until	7 18	7 29	each hour	35	41	47	53	59	5	11	17	23	29	until	1111	1121
OLD STEINE	6 28	6 47		7 30	7 41		47	53	59	5	11	17	23	29	35	41		1123	1133

WEEKDAYS — MIDWINTER (For period of operation see Page 1).

	a.m.	a.m.		p.m.	p.m.									p.m.	p.m.	p.m.	
OLD STEINE	6 3	6 22	then every	7 5	7 14	then at these	26	38	50	2	14		1050	11 2	11 8	...
FIVEWAYS	6 14	6 33	7 minutes	7 16	7 25	minutes past	37	49	1	13	25		11 1	1113	1119	...
BEACONSFIELD VILLAS	6 16	6 35	until	7 18	7 31	each hour	43	55	7	19	31	until	11 7	1115	1121	...
OLD STEINE	6 28	6 47		7 30	7 43		55	7	19	31	43		1119	1127	1133	...

SUNDAYS — WINTER (For period of operation see Page 1).

	a.m.	a.m.														p.m.			
OLD STEINE	......	9 16	then at these	22	28	34	40	46	52	58	4	10	16				1058	...	...
FIVEWAYS	......	9 27	minutes past	33	39	45	51	57	3	9	15	21	27				11 9	...	...
BEACONSFIELD VILLAS	9 17	9 29	each hour	35	42	47	53	59	5	11	17	23	29	until			1111	...	...
OLD STEINE	9 29	9 41		47	53	59	5	11	17	23	29	35	41				1123	...	...

SUNDAYS — MIDWINTER (For period of operation see Page 1).

	a.m.	a.m.										p.m.	p.m.	p.m.					
OLD STEINE	......	9 14	then at these	26	38	50	2	14			1038	1050	1058	...	...		...	...
FIVEWAYS	......	9 27	minutes past	39	51	3	15	27			1051	11 1	11 9	...	...		...	...
BEACONSFIELD VILLAS	9 19	9 31	each hour	43	55	7	19	31	until		1055	11 3	1111	...	...		...	...
OLD STEINE	9 31	9 43		55	7	19	31	43			11 7	1115	1123	...	...		...	...

88. Further down Ditchling Road at the St Saviour's Church stop, no. 25 should have applied the coasting brake before moving off, passing under the feeders and descending the steep 1 in 9 gradient to the Open Market. (David Bradley)

89. It was a Ministry of Transport requirement that the coasting brake should be applied on the section of Ditchling Road that no. 49 is seen descending in order to limit its speed to 12 mph. The trolleybus is crossing the A27 junction and is about to join up with the route 42 / 44 wires from Viaduct Road. Unusually no. 49 carries a front advertisement for "MB Motors" that does not extend as far as the destination box. (W.J.Haynes / Southdown Enthusiasts Club)

90. On another warm day in Brighton, passengers on Corporation no. 31 will not appreciate the roof ventilators having been panelled over as it stands next to one of the many brick built shelters at the Open Market stop on its way to the Aquarium. On the right of the picture, behind the trees is The Level where there is an interesting tram-type shelter. The wires along Union Road, where the car is, were retained to the end of the system for access to Lewes Road Garage. (Surfleet Negative coll.)

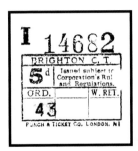

91. The buildings of Waterloo Place seen in the background here have been demolished and replaced by the Phoenix Arts Association Gallery and Workshops. The last of the Corporation AEC trolleybuses, no. 44 which entered service in May 1940 is about to begin the long climb out of town to Hollingbury. (D.Clark)

PRESTON DROVE – SURRENDEN ROAD –
BRAYBON AVENUE – CARDEN AVENUE –
HOLLINGBURY

92. Corporation no. 17 turns into Preston Drove under the curves from Beaconsfield Villas on the final extension of the system to Hollingbury, opened on 12th August 1951. The driver is making use of the illuminated semaphore indicator, but there does not seem to be any traffic around to indicate to! Trolleybuses on routes 26A/46A used the wires turning east into Preston Drove. As a child I distinctly remember travelling past this junction in

the car on the way to London and wondering why the trolleybus wires went into and out of Beaconsfield Villas, but did not continue straight down Preston Drove. (C.Carter)

93. Just down the road, the 46 trolleybus route left Preston Drove and turned into the leafy dual carriageway of Surrenden Road. No. 34 is making this move on 27th May 1961. With about four weeks to the end of the system, the nearside advertisement has been painted out and no. 34 has a unique number only nearside route indicator in place of the usual number and intermediate destination information. (At one time this trolleybus carried number only route indicators in all three boxes.) Today, a pedestrian crossing exists on Preston Drove about where the Austin A30 saloon is parked on the left. (L.W.Rowe)

94. Corporation trolleybus no. 42 is seen on the morning of 2nd August 1951 during the Board of Trade inspection of the Hollingbury extension of route 46. Public service began ten days later. The trolleybus is seen passing the playing fields of Varndean Grammar School for Boys in Surrenden Road along the dual carriageway specially built for the trolleybuses. (Brighton Herald Ltd)

95. The hill climbing capabilities of trolleybuses could be shown off to full advantage on Brighton's hills, and no better place to do this was on this steep section of Braybon Avenue. No. 30 is captured on full power under the double bracket arm suspension. Replacement motorbuses crawled up this section in the 1960s and 1970s and although modern buses keep to a good pace, they make a lot of noise. (J.Copland / C.W.Routh)

96. The photographer has chosen a superb location to capture no. 43 on film. At the bus stop a further twelve passengers are waiting to board and experience the silent operation of the trolleybus on Braybon Avenue. The school playing fields can be seen in the middle distance along with the Ladies Mile Clock Tower. Powers to operate trolleybuses to this point were obtained but never implemented. In the far distance are the rolling Sussex Chalk Downs. (P.D.Williams coll.)

97. Carden Avenue bisects the Patcham (left) and Hollingbury (right) estates. No. 29 is making its way along Carden Avenue with its grassy banks on a mid-afternoon journey into Brighton. The traction poles, although no more than ten years old look in need of painting. The last three street traction poles from Brighton trolleybus routes were removed from Carden Avenue at the beginning of 2003. (David Bradley)

98. The Hollingbury turning circle at the junction of Carden Avenue and Carden Hill can be seen in this view. No. 6 has arrived at the Carden Hill terminus (just out of shot on the right) from the Aquarium on route 26; the blind display has now been changed to show details for route 46 and it is returning to the Aquarium. The two routes were circular services and the turning circle was used only for peak-hour workings on route 26. A 500-yard extension of the wiring into the Crowhurst Road Industrial Estate from this turning circle was authorised, but never built. (D.A.Thompson)

99. It was unusual for Company trolleybuses to work on routes 26 / 46, but here no. 343 is seen on a peak-hour extra working of route 26 on 9th September 1957 and is using the turning circle facility at the Hollingbury terminus. The line of the kerb showing where trolleybuses turned can still be seen in 2005. (J.C.Gillham)

HOLLINGBURY – CARDEN HILL – DITCHLING ROAD – FIVEWAYS

100. The smartly dressed conductor, wearing his leather moneybag and "Ultimate" ticket machine has alighted from no. 42. This fine view was taken on 17th June 1961 at the bottom of Carden Hill, the terminus of route 26. Before departure, the destination and number blinds will need to be turned to display information for the 46 route that the trolleybus will use to return to the Aquarium. Neither bus shelter remains, but trees and bushes have grown to the left of the flats and houses. (L.W.Rowe)

| 26 | OLD STEINE — FIVEWAYS — HOLLINGBURY (Carden Avenue)
Via Royal Pavilion, Grand Parade, Victoria Garden, The Level, Ditchling Road, Fiveways, Municipal Golf Course, Carden Hill, Carden Avenue. | 26 |

WEEKDAYS — WINTER (For period of operation see Page I).

		a.m. a.m. a.m.		p.m. p.m.		p.m.	
OLD STEINE	dep.	5 12 5 35 6 32	and every	7 8 7 12	then at these	24 36 48 0 12	1 12	* To Open Market
FIVE WAYS	,,	5 21 5 46 6 43	7 minutes	7 19 7 23	minutes past	35 47 59 11 23 until	1 23	and Lewes Road
HOLLINGBURY	arr.	5 30 5 55 6 52	until	7 28 7 32	each hour	44 56 8 20 32	1 132	Garage.

		a.m. a.m. a.m.	and	p.m. p.m.	then at			p.m. p.m. p.m. p.m. p.m. p.m. p.m.
HOLLINGBURY	dep.	5 30 5 55 6 29	every	7 19 7 29	these mins.	41 53 5 17 29		1053 1056 11 1 11 8 113 1120 1125 ......
FIVE WAYS	,,	5 38 6 3 6 38	7 mins.	7 29 7 38	past	50 2 14 26 38 until	11 21 5 1110 117 1122 1129 1134 ......
OLD STEINE	arr.	5 49 6 14 6 49	until	7 40 7 49	each hour	1 13 25 37 49	1113 * * * * * * ......

WEEKDAYS — MIDWINTER (For period of operation see Page I).

			p.m.			p.m. p.m.	
OLD STEINE	dep.		7 8	then at these	20 32 44 56 8	p.m. p.m.	....
FIVE WAYS	,,	NORMAL WINTER SERVICE UNTIL	7 19	these mins.	31 43 55 7 19 until	11 7 1123	....
HOLLINGBURY	arr.		7 28	each hour	40 52 4 16 28	1116 1132	....

			p.m. p.m. p.m.			p.m. p.m.	
HOLLINGBURY	dep.		7 19 7 26 7 37	then at these	49 1 13 25 37	1049 1058‡	......
FIVE WAYS	,,	NORMAL WINTER SERVICE UNTIL	7 29 7 35 7 46	mins. past	58 10 22 34 46 until	1058 11 7	......
OLD STEINE	arr.		7 40 7 46 7 57	each hour	9 21 33 45 57	11 9 1118	......

‡then approximately every 6 minutes to Five Ways, Open Market and Lewes Road Garage until 11.25 p.m.

SUNDAYS — WINTER (See Page I).

		a.m.			p.m.
OLD STEINE	dep.	9 0	and at these	0 12 24 36 48	11 0
FIVE WAYS		9 11	mins. past	11 23 35 47 59 until	1111
HOLLINGBURY		9 20	each hour	20 32 44 56 8	1120

		a.m.			p.m.
HOLLINGBURY		8 41	and at these	5 17 29 41 53	1049§
FIVE WAYS		8 49	mins. past	14 26 38 50 2 until	1050
OLD STEINE		9 0	each hour	25 37 49 1 13	11 1

§Then 10.51 and approximately every 6 minutes until 11.27 p.m. Five Ways, Open Market and Lewes Road Garage.

SUNDAYS — MIDWINTER (For period of operation see Page I).

		a.m. a.m.	then at		p.m. p.m.	
OLD STEINE		9 0 9 20	these	32 44 56 8 20	1044 11 0	....
FIVE WAYS		9 11 9 31	mins.	43 55 7 19 31 until	1055 1111	....
HOLLINGBURY		9 20 9 40	past each	52 4 16 28 40	11 4 1120	....
			hour			

		a.m. a.m.	then at		p.m. p.m. p.m. p.m.	
HOLLINGBURY		8 41 9 1	these	13 25 37 49 1	1049 11 1 4 1110 1120	
FIVE WAYS		8 49 9 10	mins.	22 34 46 58 10 until	1058 1110 1113 1119 1129	
OLD STEINE		9 0 9 21	past each	33 45 57 9 21	11 9 * * * *	
			hour			

* To Open Market and Lewes Road Garage.

101. Corporation trolleybus no. 25 is beginning the long climb of Carden Hill through the Hollingbury estate. The lollipop lady is in position to see children leaving Carden Infant and Junior School across the road, which was finished with distinctive pink chippings. The split-windscreen Morris Minor travelling down the hill has an interesting registration plate, LCD 53 – being one number after the final Corporation trolleybus, LCD 52. The open space on the right has been built on. (C.Bennett and M.Jenkins, Online Transport Archive.)

102. There was an overhead line problem when this photograph was taken at the top of Carden Hill. Fortunately an inspector has come to the aid of the conductor and no. 5 should be able to free wheel down the hill towards the terminus and continue with its journey after reaching the next section. The ultimate destination indicator has already been changed for the return journey (on route 46). Compare this rear view with that of the Company trolleybus shown in photograph 78. No. 5 has a projecting rear destination box, the red rear lamp adjacent to the registration plate, a paler "stopping" sign, two rear reflectors at the bottom of the bodywork and a rectangular advertisement in place of the circular variety on Company trolleybuses.
(J.H.Jones / Southdown Enthusiasts Club)

103. The Larkfield Way turning circle seen in this view was used as the terminus for routes 26 and 46 from 28th November 1948 until 22nd March 1949. From the following day trolleybuses on these routes were extended down Carden Hill to Carden Avenue and the facility was used only occasionally. Trolleybus no. 34 is turning out of Carden Hill into Woodbourne Avenue after its long climb through the estate. Both the brick bus shelter and the red telephone kiosk have been replaced by modern equivalents. (C.Bennett and M.Jenkins, Online Transport Archive)

104. This view shows the original 1939 "Golf Links" terminus of routes 26 and 46 in Ditchling Road at the junction with Surrenden Road. In 2005, the kerb line of the turning circle still remains, as does the recently repainted tram shelter, part of which can be seen in this view at the front of no. 34. The wires were extended up the hill beyond the reservoir from 28th November 1948 to Larkfield Way on the edge of the developing Hollingbury estate. (P.D.Williams coll.)

105. Corporation no. 29 accelerates after passing under the feeder in this springtime photograph of Ditchling Road on its way to Fiveways and the town. Behind the trees on the right is Hollingbury Park with its bowling greens and tennis courts. The stop that the trolleybus has just left is that at Varndean Grammar School for Girls. (C.Bennett and M.Jenkins, Online Transport Archive)

FINALE – THE LAST DAYS OF THE TROLLEYBUSES

106. This view of Company no. 340 turning out of St James's Street shows an interesting variety of 1950s transport. From left to right are:- a 1948 Southdown Guy Arab III with Northern Counties 54-seat bodywork on route 13; 1959 Brighton Corporation Leyland PD 2/37, no. 51 (WCD 51) with Weymann 61-seat bodywork on route 42; 1939 Brighton, Hove and District AEC 661T, no. 340 (CPM 61) with Weymann 54-seat bodywork on route 42; and one of the later Brighton, Hove and District Bristol KSW6Gs with rain-shields built in the period 1954-6 with Eastern Coachworks 60-seat bodywork on route 3. For a few days in March 1959, motorbuses nos. 51 and 53 ran alongside trolleybuses to give drivers practice with the manual gearboxes – Stage 1 of the conversion programme is imminent. (F.W.Ivey)

107. Looking rather battered from damage sustained just before closure, no. 1 stands in front of no. 27 at the Aquarium, Old Steine terminus on the last afternoon of trolleybus operation in Brighton - Friday, 30th June 1961. The board, complete with the Borough of Brighton's coat-of-arms, is carried on its front while the side advertisement panel reads 1939 Brighton Trolley Buses 1961. Late in the evening, this trolleybus closed the system. One of the replacement forward-entrance Leyland PD2/37 motorbuses can be seen on the extreme left. (Surfleet Negative coll.)

108. Brighton's last trolleybus is seen on the forecourt of Lewes Road Garage with its interior lights ablaze on the evening of 30th June 1961. It has left public service and is being prepared for its final run. Soon its guests would arrive and no. 1 would depart on its final journey to the Aquarium and back to complete Stage 2 of the conversion programme. In the background, an AEC Regent III stands next to some of the 1959 batch of rear entrance Leyland PD2/37s bought to replace trolleybuses at Stage 1 of the conversion programme. (T.M.Russell)

109. The last public service trolleybus, no. 36 operated the 11.3 pm. from the Aquarium on route 46 to Hollingbury. Here it changed to route 26, operating the 11.25 pm. journey back into town and then to the Garage as a 48. On this occasion, instead of operating from the Open Market direct to the Garage as per the timetable, it completed the circle and continued to the Aquarium before heading home. No. 36 has arrived at Lewes Road Garage where it has unloaded its passengers. Within a few minutes, privately hired no. 34 with no. 1 immediately behind it would arrive and close the Brighton trolleybus system. (M.Dryhurst)

ROLLING STOCK

110. The first trolleybuses to enter service between May 1939 and May 1940 were forty-four Brighton Corporation Transport AEC 661Ts with Weymann 54-seat bodies. They carried fleet numbers 1-44 (FUF 1-44) and were withdrawn in the period 1957-1961. This view shows no. 39, looking as if it has had a repaint, including the reversion to having a cream roof but still carrying Wartime white paint on its mudguards. The trolleybus in front has a grey roof and shows off the curve of the Weymann bodywork well. No. 39 was one of the first Corporation trolleybuses to be withdrawn in 1957 and is seen at the Aquarium, Old Steine terminus.
(W.J.Haynes / Southdown Enthusiasts Club)

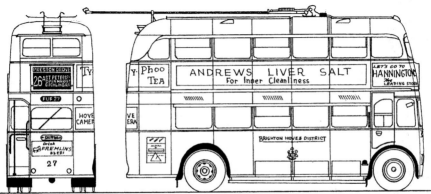

K.A.Allbon.

BRIGHTON TROLLEYBUS

A.E.C./ WEYMANN

BRIGHTON CORPORATION
TRANSPORT
Nos. 1 - 44
1939 - 1961

BRIGHTON HOVE & DISTRICT
OMNIBUS Co., Ltd.
Nos. 6340 - 6347
1945 - 1959

The Company vehicles differed
from the Corporation buses in
having flush destination boxes,
& lacked the front wheel hub
caps & Brighton crest on the
side panels. The rear lamp was
at waist rail, rather than cant
rail level.

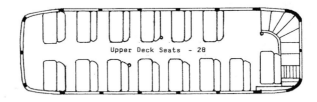

Upper Deck Seats - 28

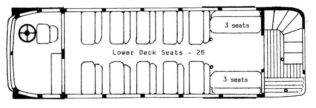

Lower Deck Seats - 26

3 seats

3 seats

Scale:

Metres
0   1   2

0 1 2 3 4 5 6 7
Feet

111. Brighton, Hove and District Omnibus Company Limited bought eight almost identical AEC 661T trolleybuses with Weymann 54-seat bodies. They carried fleet numbers 6340-7, the "Tilling 6000" prefix being dropped after 1955. They were originally registered BPN 340-7, but these were surrendered as entry into service was delayed by the start of World War II. They were re-registered CPM 61/62/53/375/101/102/521 and 997, entering service between 1st January 1945 and 1st May 1946. All were officially withdrawn on 24th March 1959. No. 6345 is seen outside Weymann's body factory at Addlestone prior to delivery, carrying its original registration plate BPN 345. It was re-registered CPM 102 when it finally entered service during the early months of 1945. (R.Marshall)

112. This view shows the upper deck of Corporation no. 36 looking towards the rear emergency exit, which was hinged at the bottom. Four of the Widney "Aero" half-drop moving windows can be seen. These were framed in chromium-plated channels with stainless steel racks and handles. The ceiling is covered with Alhambrinal material. The 20-watt bulbs in the stainless steel roof lamps were of Taw manufacture. The seats, well worn by the time this photograph was taken in March

1959, had Dean's tubular steel framework with stainless steel top rail incorporating corner grab handles. Cushions were built up on Dunlopillo rubber cases and the complete seats were trimmed in comfortable Lister moquette and Connolly leather. The Ashanco ventilators can also be seen between the lamps while part of the rectangular mirror to aid the conductor can be seen behind the rear left seat. (J.C.Gillham)

113. Downstairs, the trolleybuses were finished in a similar fashion. The polished wooden cabinet contains Brighton, Hove and District Transport Trolleybus Fare Tables. To the right of the cabinet Easter Services, 1959 Traffic Arrangements leaflets are hanging, for this view was taken on 22nd March 1959. The notice on the right declares that the seating capacity of Corporation trolleybus no. 33

is 54 with 28 seats in the upper saloon and 26 seats in the lower saloon. That on the rear platform states that when all seats are occupied 8 passengers are allowed to stand on the lower deck. There are also plenty of internal paper advertisements stuck to the windows, but the usual advertisements for "Vokins" behind the longitudinal seats appear to be missing. (J.C.Gillham)

114. Looking towards the front of the same vehicle, a polished wooden cabinet can be seen, which incorporated a central bell push. Period advertisements are displayed within the cabinet, while above it is a "No Smoking" sign. "Bus No. 33" is displayed above the advertisement for Albert Brick - a local glazing contractor. The window behind the driver could be slid back to allow communication between the crew - the blind was usually lowered at dusk. (J.C.Gillham)

115. This view shows the interior of Company no. 6340 for comparison when it was at the East Anglia Transport Museum in 1996. While similar to that of the Corporation, there were

some differences and they can be seen here. What can't be seen is that the interiors of Corporation trolleybuses were green whereas those of the Company were red; the moquette used on Company trolleybuses was particularly itchy to those like me wearing short trousers. The white ceiling may not have been so artistic, but gave a much brighter interior than on Corporation vehicles. (M.J.Stedman)

116. Brighton, Hove and District placed three BUT 9611T trolleybuses with Weymann 56-seat bodies in service from 24th March 1948. They carried fleet numbers 6391-3, later 391-3 and were registered DNJ 992-4. They were withdrawn ahead of the trolleybus replacement programme in the period 30th January 1959 to 28th February 1959 and sold to Bournemouth Corporation Transport in March 1959 where they became nos 292-4 in that fleet. No. 392 (DNJ 993) is seen in the mid-day summer sunshine at Black Rock, running along the fifty yards or so of Marine Drive before turning inland for its return journey to Seven Dials. This was the only place where trolleybuses ran along Brighton's seafront. At one time trolleybuses terminated here on the main A259 cliff-top coastal road east of Brighton. Behind the photographer, at the bottom of the cliff, was the popular Black Rock open-air swimming pool and the shingle beach. Black Rock is the site of Brighton Marina today – the swimming pool, closed in 1978, remains derelict in 2005. The photograph was taken on 28th June 1953 when unlike today, the trolleybus had the road to itself. (D.L.Williams)

117. Brighton Corporation bought eight BUT 9611T chassis and had six fitted with Weymann 56- seat bodies. They were almost identical to the BH&D trolleybuses, carried fleet numbers 45-50 and were registered HUF 45-50, entering service between April and June 1948. They were all withdrawn in December 1958 and sold for further service in February 1959. Nos.45-8 went to Bournemouth where

they became nos 288-91, while nos 49 and 50 (which were fitted with English Electric motors) went to Bradford Corporation where they became nos 802 and 803. No. 45 is seen at the Aquarium, Old Steine terminus waiting its departure time to Preston Drove. (D.A.Jones / London Trolleybus Preservation Soc.)

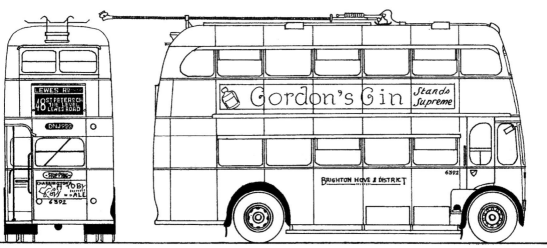

K.A.Allbon.

BRIGHTON TROLLEYBUS

B.U.T./ WEYMANN

BRIGHTON CORPORATION
TRANSPORT
Nos. 45 - 52
1948 - 1959

BRIGHTON HOVE & DISTRICT
OMNIBUS Co., Ltd.
Nos. 6391 - 6393
1948 - 1959

The Corporation buses differed
from the Company vehicles in
having front wheel nut rings,
& Brighton crest on the side
panels. All these buses were
sold for further service in
1959, to Bournemouth, Bradford
and Maidstone.

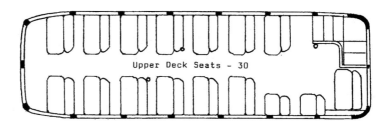

Upper Deck Seats - 30

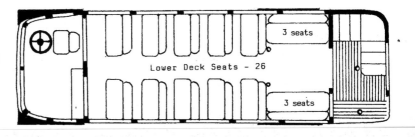

Lower Deck Seats - 26

3 seats

3 seats

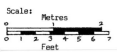

Scale:

Metres
0   1   2

Feet
0 1 2 3 4 5 6 7

118. The final two BUT 9611T trolleybus chassis were sent to Weymann for fitting with 56-seat bodies in September 1951. Registered LCD 51-2, they carried fleet numbers 51-2, but did not enter service until March 1953. They were withdrawn in December 1958, being sold to Maidstone Corporation in February 1959 for further use. No. 52 stands in the mid-day sunshine on the outer set of wires at the Aquarium, Old Steine terminus. (John Fozard / Bob Mack coll.)

119. Brighton Corporation owned a number of tower wagons, mobile cranes and a tractor. One of the tower wagons was Dennis 141 (BUF 679) which was converted from a dustcart during the war and still exists. It is seen here at the Larkfield Way turning circle in Hollingbury with workmen repairing the overhead. No. 19, which has had its blinds changed for the return journey into Brighton may well follow no. 5, just visible in front and be pushed onto the slope of Carden Hill. (J.H.Jones / Southdown Enthusiasts Club)

POSTSCRIPT

120. This last view, taken on 19th September 1963, is of J.Light's yard at Southerham, near Lewes, where most of Brighton's trolleybus fleet was scrapped. In front of the Southdown bus on the left, is no. 19, while behind it is no. 32. Almost in the centre of the photograph, carrying a blue advertisement for BTS Television, is Brighton's last trolleybus – no. 1. Some of the trolleybuses spent longer here than they did in service, the last being broken up in 1985. (B.Johnson)

MP **Middleton Press**

EVOLVING THE ULTIMATE RAIL ENCYCLOPEDIA

Easebourne Lane, Midhurst, West Sussex.
GU29 9AZ   Tel:01730 813169

www.middletonpress.co.uk email:info@middletonpress.co.uk
A-0 906520   B-1 873793   C-1 901706   D-1 904474

OOP Out of Print at time of printing - Please check current availability   **BROCHURE AVAILABLE SHOWING NEW TITLES**